A FAR COUNTRY HERE

A Far Country Here

George Hobson

Foreword by John Paris

WIPF & STOCK · Eugene, Oregon

A FAR COUNTRY HERE

Copyright © 2021 George Hobson. All rights reserved. Except for brief quotations in critical publications or reviews, no part of this book may be reproduced in any manner without prior written permission from the publisher. Write: Permissions, Wipf and Stock Publishers, 199 W. 8th Ave., Suite 3, Eugene, OR 97401.

Resource Publications
An Imprint of Wipf and Stock Publishers
199 W. 8th Ave., Suite 3
Eugene, OR 97401

www.wipfandstock.com

PAPERBACK ISBN: 978-1-6667-2506-3
HARDCOVER ISBN: 978-1-6667-2037-2
EBOOK ISBN: 978-1-6667-2038-9

AUGUST 31, 2021

For Richard Hays, dear friend for fifty years,
yoke-fellow in Christ's service,
peerless Biblical scholar.

Contents

Foreword by John Paris | ix
Acknowledgements | xv

Part I

Lost *(Montana, 1944)* | 3
The Gold Coin | 5
The Antique Moon | 6
Morning | 8
Found | 9
Named | 10
Growing Up | 12

Part II

Indian Summer | 15
Crayons | 16
Autumn | 18
Fall | 20
Moments | 22
White | 24
Winter's Last Battle | 27
Harbingers | 29
The Daily Circle | 32
Rain | 33
The Hollyhocks | 36
Pride | 37

Part III

Cloud Sequences | 41

Part IV

The Plaque on the Bench | 49
For Richard Hays | 50
Friends | 52
The Friends Have Gone | 58
Waiting | 61
The Temptation of Darkness | 64
Pour Albert, Mon Frère Bien-Aimé | 67
Grief | 69
Clovis | 71
The Canvas | 73

Part V

Harold the King | 77
Crater Lake | 83
"There is a World Elsewhere" | 86
Stampede | 89
A Far Country Here | 90
The Ridge | 92

Part VI

A Far Isle | 99
The Yellow Rose of England | 105
The Figure at the End of the Pier | 111
Bees Among the Plums | 114
Old Man Under the Night | 116
The Little Green Vessel | 118

Foreword

OPENING A BOOK OF POETRY is not quite like anything else. With a work of fiction we expect a possibility, then a problem, and the promise of some outworking from the first page through the consummation of the plot. But with this kind of book one never knows just what he will find in that first poem, or the next, or the next. In George Hobson's work, you will meet a creator-interpreter who speaks with intimacy about the entire universe in those places where its life and his own, and ours – and our Creator – all intersect.

For creatures in a fallen world, this often means the great themes of loss and restoration, grief and comfort, defeat and transfiguration considered and reconsidered within the flow of time and the irruptions of memory – but, like the Psalms, almost always ending redemptively. The few poems without that resolution only prepare us more acutely to receive our next gift of renewed, living hope. Hobson looks at what can be a very bleak world with unflinching rectitude, but never without profound feeling that is the heartache of God Himself. And illuminating it all, sometimes from a great height, sometimes encompassing us, is the *Shekinah*, the shining presence of the Lord Jesus Christ reminding us of His sacrifice, His utterly faithful love and the certainty of eternal life in Him. I can testify with great affection for George (and his lovely wife Victoria – my oldest friends) that this awareness infuses him as well as his writing, welling up from love and transparency before his Lord and us.

Foreword

This makes for a vulnerability of great power and tenderness. I urge you to take in all that is disclosed from the heart, the depths of one man's heart, for example in "The Figure at the End of the Pier," where the poet speaks to the little boy he once was: "As a child, you didn't have a family; As a man, I didn't have a family either." We meet the same little boy on a bare wooden porch on the dusty plains of Montana, and an aside tells us all.

> *Water in these parts is frail, out of place;*
> *It doesn't speak the local language;*
> *It sinks quickly into the hot soil,*
> *Leaving only stains by the pump*
> *And awkward memories of wetness.*

Not that near-tragedy, however ennobled with his transmutation, is all this poet has to give. No one is more eager to reveal Nature in its exquisite, often humorous minutiae as well as its immensities. And there is high drama, sometimes of wonderful ambiguity that mixes mundane phenomena with the transcendent. In this, Hobson is a master of staging and personification, enabling us to discern the delightful interplay of God's creatures (including their human pets or counterparts) as he parades them through their environments. Their animations can reveal quirks, beauties, and depths of personality far better than a logical dissection ever could.

And what do you make of the following, quoted in its entirety?

> *Body-builder clouds flex their muscles.*
> *They tower and glower.*
> *Considering contemptuously the soft hills, they gloat.*
> *They preen, boast, growl,*
> *Smirk, snicker, stalk.*
> *They will douse the hills,*
> *Drown the land;*
> *Their sword, wind, will rip trees,*
> *Uproot orchards,*
> *Destroy what men have made.*
> *The sky will crack,*
> *Day will turn to night.*
> *Having shot their wad,*

Foreword

Having strained and strutted,
Having roared and bellowed,
The body-building bar-bell toting bumptious clouds
Will be spent.
Their bombast vented,
They will deflate like tires
And hobble bumpity-bump over the hills, muttering.
The sky will clear,
Then the sun will come out.
The blue day won't even remember the braggarts.
The green hills,
Made of rock under their soft curves,
Will laugh.

The title of the poem is *Pride*. Many Christian poets have found ways to excoriate haughty abusiveness with verse that brings it right against our face, meaning to make its hideousness utterly (and understandably) revolting. With an amusing portrayal of Nature, diverting all by itself, Hobson takes up what may be the ultimate weapon against pride – comic ridicule – and shows it for the pathetic posturing it is, and the triumph of a creation content to be what her Maker has made, immortally resilient and literally having the last laugh.

Having grown up in New York City but with seasons on his father's ranch in British Columbia and occasionally fighting fires in the forestry service, contrasted with visits to his grandmother in Paris and study of the French language in Lausanne, Hobson has more than the usual range of living to draw on. That along with later life that shuttled him between Oxford and Paris and a remote hamlet in the French countryside, and then found him teaching theology in seminaries in five developing countries. He spins yarns drawn from the far west plains and mountains, and a country ballad to go with them; he pulls us into the darkness and pain of a cityscape. He can move from being matter-of-fact to hermetic and shadowy, stark and violent, tender and nuanced. I will not spoil your adventure but will leave it to you to discover the exceptional diversity of form, from sonnet to (almost, but not really) free verse. There is often fierce energy in words gyrating, piling up incongruously and colliding; then delicate discretion with something too fragile to be touched, only beheld. And as you get to know Hobson's poetry in this and his other volumes, you will become acquainted with what I call his 'nocturnes.' They are his frequent ventures into the night, where a special musing seems to take hold of him as he contemplates, by turns, scary intergalactic vastness, whimsy, and eternal glory.

> *Rise, heart!*
> *See the young moon up there on her deckchair*
> *Surveying the fecundity of stars,*
> *A playground of children squealing with light.*

Finally, consider George Hobson's work in this sense: on occasion we turn to the poetry of a Dickinson or Herbert because we hunger to hear their familiar but unique and utterly consistent voice fully as much as what they say with it. There are times when no one else will do; and for that very reason, there are other times it would not enter our head to read them. I wonder if you will find a poet in English who exceeds this one for sheer versatility, for a range of expression in voice and content where every manifestation is authentic no matter the form. It is not that Hobson is looking for ways to be different but for the way into the heart of what must be conveyed with fidelity to its inherent life, ineluctable structure, tone, accent, affect. It is simply a matter of what serves the message, as if he has not found it but it has found him. His capacity to become one with the subject ensures that our experience of it will be as vivid as his own encounter, without any of that self-consciousness of the artificer who turns what should be a moment of immediacy into mere analysis. Hobson's span of poetic engagement is extraordinary, and he enables the reader to partake with him fully in it. Whether opening up the subtle and often overlooked details of Nature, or compressing the vast reaches of the galaxies, or drawing forth insight from inchoate portions of memory, these poems indeed bring a far country here.

This remarkable variety of expression in every collection of his work means that some poems will not appeal to you, and that may be that. But beware: I have found that a poem I turned from with just a "Hmmm…" on first reading arrested and held me when I happened on it a few months later. Was it a mood? Had I grown a bit more perceptive and open? Was it that on this occasion, unawares, I'd settled down and given it the full attentiveness all good poetry deserves? (There is, of course, excellent poetry that almost from the first syllable grabs the reader and interprets itself to him effortlessly, and George Hobson has written much of that, too, as we have just seen.) So be careful not to deprive yourself.

Every art form has its differing appeal and access. When it comes to music, most of us listen in our heads but aurally as well; how often do we think to give ourselves the same pleasure with poetry? That is, passages from these poems will lodge in your mind and some of them will become rooted in your heart, and you will be blessed as they come up before you. But do keep the hard copy nearby also (how many books of poetry do you have on your bedside table?). Pick it up and browse, letting it speak to you and nourish you along with those other things of beauty and truthfulness you have placed around you, things that remind you of their Presence and Source. It will add to the sum of your life.

John Paris
Senior Consultant in
Executive Development and Organizational Effectiveness

Acknowledgements

With gratitude to my close friends Mindy Braithwaite, Sylvie Botétémé, and Eliane and René Tixier, whose devotion to me and to my beloved Victoria, and whose support for my work as a poet, have sustained me during long years of trial. I am also indebted to Patrice Rochereau for his appreciation of my poetry and his unceasing encouragement to me as a writer.

Part I

Lost (Montana, 1944)

The color of the prairie in Montana is dust.
On the porch of the house on the plains, no green
Shoots up, no yellow blooms, no pink
Splashes roses on the weathered siding.
Sky-blue is abstract here,
A dream beyond the dust of time,
Beyond all dry plains
Painted on the human soul.
Water in these parts is frail, out of place;
It doesn't speak the local language;
It sinks quickly into the hot soil,
Leaving only stains by the pump
And awkward memories of wetness.

Hear the cry of the dust.
Hear the cry of the child rolling marbles alone
On the porch of the house in the prairie
(No other cries can be heard,
No one is anywhere to be seen):
Marbles of glass that glint in sunlight
And click in the silence of the air.
The round balls cut straight lines
Like jets painting contrails on the dream of blue.
They are red and green, orange, violet,
All the colors of the spectrum.
A beautiful green one,
The color of fern,
Disappears suddenly down a crack in the floorboards
And is lost.
(Underneath the house, creatures slither in the dark;
One does not go looking for things
That have disappeared under the house.)
Rage consumes the child,

Pain freezes him;
Fire and ice capture his heart.
Bitterly, desperately, defiantly,
He rolls the other marbles down the crack.
"I'm lost!" his soul shrieks.
"I'm gone down into darkness!"
And: "Henceforth I'll create my own world out of nothing."

The soil in which pride roots is dry.
Rejection breeds rejection.
It hasn't rained in these parts for years.

The Gold Coin

In the gutter of the wet street I found a coin
Buried deep in sodden leaves by the drain.
Head down, despairing, I was on my way to join
The lost souls, when a glint of gold in the rain
Caught my eye. A round edge of the coin peeped
Out like the sun's curved corner from the clouds,
And I, reverently parting the black leaves heaped
About, drew it from its water-laden shrouds.
An ancient piece it was, and that proud head
Which once was carved upon its golden face
Was gone, rubbed smooth like his memory, long dead.
Yet still the metal glittered, offering praise
To him who forged the bright coin in time past.
Renewed, I shaped my own image in its gold,
I, creator and created, and fresh hope fast
Blossomed in my heart, which sorrow had turned cold.

The Antique Moon

The limbs of the plane trees that grow
By the banks of the river were lopped off
One May morning. I was young then,
And I remember well how it was:
When the bark covered the wounds,
The ends of the limbs were like fists;
In the night the trees creaked by the river
And shook their stumpy arms at the moon.

Power lines that ran by the river's edge
Had to be protected, so the limbs
Of the trees that threatened to nest in the wires
Had to be cut. The twigs were pruned,
As well as the dangerous green buds;
The leafless branches left behind
Twisted from the trunks in bunches,
Like the writhing snakes of Medusa.

The soft moon that climbed the sky
And shone on the mangled plane trees
Was turned to stone. I was abroad
In the city that fearful night,
And I remember well how it was:
Darkness fell upon the lovers
Kissing in the moonlit streets,
And their tongues turned into knives.

I left home soon after, for life
In the city was only pain: the lips
Of those who dared to love were bloody.
Since then, in my dreams, I have glimpsed
The lost moon, floating in memories;

But in the cities where pruned plane trees
Line the elegant avenues,
I have not found the antique moon.

Morning

In the blue day I run into amazing morning!
Spill down ruby mountains like foxglove in bloom!
Bolt out of thunder-clouds like lightning!
Plunge into boulder-bearing rivers heedless!

I sit in foreign cities writing poems, heedless
That words aren't welcome in the world's loud morning
Unless they make our urban deserts bloom
With money-trees that dazzle night-bound eyes like lightning.

History's horror on the mind's rim like lightning
Over mountains, the menace of it, shimmers, I heedless
Of dead-end dark and the dull cast morning
Wears in most men's eyes, who have no hope to bloom.

Young, and like all young men everywhere, I bloom
In hope and hope to bloom, ignore the double lightning
Of my sin and mortal limits, blind boy, heedless
That already brown blight singes the leaves of morning.

O hope rooted in men's hearts like forks of lightning
In the planet's night: O high hope of the great bloom
Of Life: you do shine, you must shine, beyond our quick-gone
   morning!

Found

My Lord, you've found me!
You've turned my mourning into laughter!
My loneliness you've filled with love!
You've forgiven my rages,
Thawed my heart,
Besieged my ugly pride!
You went down yourself into the dark
Under the old rotten house
And snatched the marble from the snakes.
How beautiful it is in the sunlight—
The color of fern.
And you've gathered the other marbles
With the green one—how bright they look!
How lovely they are all together!
You've washed them with the water of life—
Your life!
My God—thank you!

Named

When, saddened by our human plight
(We trust not God or men, from fear
Of death and time's unravelling spool),
I stand, O Lord, beneath your night
And hear the grass and tired trees
Stirring in their sleep, I feel a fool
To fret that our inveterate sin,
Yielding such disloyalty, might shake
The structures of your faithfulness.
When lightning rends the dark, and din
Of thunder claps in cloud-quake
That makes the poor heart tremble,
The breadth of your great power, Lord,
Your sway and glory, strikes my soul;
Sin's citadels encroaching on our race,
Issue of our disgrace, then cease to tower
In my mind, and fear, faith's enemy,
Is toppled from its throne and trampled down.

Yet under the turn of constellations,
The Dippers, Taurus, the precious stars
That stud the White Way's lustrous hoop,
What prompts my heart to adoration
Is not the splendor of those heavenly flames,
Not night's sweep nor the galaxy's loop
In space, but wind in the dark leaves,
Breathing on the furrowed earth, breathing
On my furrowed brow, the still voice
In the breeze whispering under the eaves
Of the universe, calling the heart harrowed
By love's impossibility, to rejoice.
Oh, not the call's content but the fact
Of it, first is wonderful—I am named!

And if named, then known, wanted, claimed.
The call itself—the Word—is the act.
Found—loved!—I stand enthralled
To hear on the night wind my name called.

Growing Up

I'm no longer young. Youth's presumptions,
When the future was a green bud, are gone.
Hopes then were expectations, sumptuous
Figures of beautiful creatures singing a song
I had no doubt they'd sing to me one day.
They've sung and sung—even to me sometimes—
But not the song I'd dreamed then, nor in the key
I'd imagined before faith came, young man flinging rhymes
On blank white sheets and brashly hiring chance
To blaze a laureled trail and clear the way
Through glens and vague valleys and along
Wild cliff-tops, beyond the steeple's chimes.
But I've grown up, and chance has proved a sham;
My hope lies all in Christ now, God's Holy Lamb.

Part II

Indian Summer

Bumble bees buzz busily
Among the dahlias;
Sparrows twitter
In the walnut trees;
Indian summer laughs
On the oak-clad hills.
The hazel shakes
Its heart-shaped leaves,
Sighing to recall
The jewelled berries
Of the elder in August.

Sheep are strung along a field
Like buttons on a waistcoat:
Chalk and teak ewes,
A stout ram.
The shepherd's patter
Lifts in the flush day
Like a memory of stars.

Lichen paints outcrops
Of old sea-beds
With hues of mustard;
In the grass a beetle rustles;
Moss in quilted strips
Bedecks the dry rock wall
Where a cat lies curled
On a stone cushion at noon.

Crayons

The colored clothespins on the plastic cord
Stretched between the plum trees
Look like rows of happy crayons
Lined up neatly in a box of air.
I take a yellow one and color
On a drawing pad
Crocuses in clustered colonies.

These are settlements on a wilderness map.

And I remember, as my flowers bloom,
That land unexplored like my empty page
Was common in an age gone by
Before space was overrun by man.

Now I color green all over,
Swathes, dashes,
Blade upon blade,
Grass, bushes.
Around my field I draw a stone wall
With gray crayon,
Then stroke in a turtle-colored yucca.
Now a terrace rises where I'm sitting,
Bounded by a thorny pyrocanthus.
On the wall's lip hang berries
Like orange suns on the world's rim.
Two bushy pines spring up from the ground,
Long cones like pendant earrings.
Then plum trees take shape, daubed with purple,
Then a cherry with crimson spots,
As if the poor tree had measles.
A spinach-colored crayon adds moss to the walls,
A scruffy acacia gets fitted with ivy.

Horizontal strokes create an orange swing,
Others make a bench of walnut wood.
A black crayon sketches metal chairs
And the frame of a glass-topped table.

Here, Fall coming, leaves drop,
Go twirling, loop, settle on the glass as on a pond,
Rest here, rest there,
On briars, on bushes,
In the needles of the green pines,
Brown, gold, rusty smudges,
The work of crayons.

I have tamed the land,
Filled the empty space.
I have tried to do it no harm,
I have loved it.
Yet a longing lingers
For the blank sheet,
The virgin page,
Unmarked by human hand.

And it will be time soon
To line up the crayons
In their box of air on the laundry line
And turn them back into clothespins
To hang up the wash.

Autumn

The leaves of the cherry trees are the color of carrots.
On the hills the oaks stand out like redheads in a crowd.
A pale mist melts along the undulating crest.

Everything is wet

The pane of our slanted bedroom window
Figures river deltas running seaward.
In the metal gutters light drops tinkle.
On our stone terrace puddles quiver.
Mahogany magnolia leaves float like canoes
In pools on the rain-riddled road.
Black-eyed Susans, butter-yellow,
Wave damp petals at the drizzling clouds.
Each rose-hip on the bush outside our door
Sports a glassy raindrop for an earring.
Althea blossoms droop on their stems
Like pink panties on a coat-rack.
In the thorny pyrocanthus behind our house
The berries glow like campfires in a forest.
Two damp doves sit huddled on a chimney,
Their heads half-buried in their feathers.

Autumn is an explosion at the red end of the spectrum.
Soon dun will take over,
Glum dun.

Winter

Color will go into hiding.
Trees will look scraggly like Beethoven's hair,
Fields will be the color of cigars.

No green.
Life will be ruminating inside the earth,
Squirreled away like nuts.

Everything will shiver

Fall

Trees are turning into fruits.
Lemons are bulging all over the hills,
Red apples, pot-bellied peaches,
Oranges, persimmons, pears—
Bulky fruits where green trees were.
What is happening?
Look—color is investing the woods,
Springing up in the forests!
On the ridges—fruits billowing!
They're spilling down the slopes—
Painted hordes!
Invasion!
We're under attack!
Fruits are taking over the hills!
To arms!

Or is it a circus?
Have I got it right?
Maybe we should dance, not shoot.
Are the fruits clowns?

Suddenly shadow falls over the earth.
Clouds growl,
Tanks of wind roll out of heaven.
Cold sneers.

And then it starts to rain leaves.
It rains leaves for a week without let-up.
Billions fall,
Clog the earth.
Leaf-lakes swamp the fields,
Bury the roads.

It's a rout.
The invasion of fruits is repulsed,
The clowns beaten back,
The trees taken prisoner.

Wind wins,
Cold wins.

All that remains on the skeletal hills
Are colorless branches and tree-trunks.

Moments

I

Here and there along the road
Thorny stems of bramble,
Bare but for clusters of small orange leaves at their tips,
Vault from the hedge's tangle high into air,
Then hang their heads in long loops, as if browsing,
Recalling, in an instant of memory,
Long-necked giraffes standing by low bushes
On an African plain.

II

Last night it snowed.
On the roadside jungle of brambles
Snow makes sinewy web-like threads of white,
As if some very large snow-secreting spider
Had labored all night long among the hedgerows
To snare and devour errant creatures,
Chiefly birds,
Who happened to alight among the briars.

III

A light snow has fallen.
It is morning.
The unshorn meadows, with long green hair, are frothy;
The ploughed fields, brown as cloves, wear woolen tops;
The houses on the hillside gleam with fresh coats of lime;

The bushy woods, bleached, are the color of walnuts.
The landscape is a newly-laid terra-cotta mosaic,
Dusted with flour.

White

You sit, there is snow falling, it falls all day,
All the stars in heaven falling all day.
You watch through the window panes and wonder
Who you are, you wonder about the snowflakes
And where they come from, what they are,
So many trillions and trillions of them.
You think of the dead of all the ages,
And perhaps the flakes are words they are speaking
To the living, words of blessing perhaps,
Whispered from heaven to your heart.

You wake, it is white everywhere, snow
Makes walls of white along the tree limbs,
Buries under white the rocks, roofs, hedges.
You rub your eyes. Is it April,
When blackthorn, like milk boiling over,
Swamps the hedgerows,
And dogwoods erupt in the fields?
No. No green now. *Cold.* This is snow.
April is a dream.

You sleep and wake. *White.*
The world is pure.
In your heart it is white too, briefly,
Before the shadow passes,
Before the vulture swoops.
Hope is a white flower blooming in the cold.

You remember days of sun, nights of moon.
Seasons turn, times turn,
There are winters, there are springs.
Where cruelty stalks, blood runs;

In gardens of mercy, water flows.
All comes, all goes.
And you, like a bird in flight,
Rise and dip,
And you go on, always you go on,
Like a bird piercing the air.
You are carried
(You didn't make your wings,
You didn't make the air),
Yet you carve your own course,
You carve your course through the seasons.

Spring will return, and winter.
The snow will melt.
The buds will break into leaf,
Brown and green will cover the earth.
Then the leaves will drop,
The snow fall,
All will be white again.
You yourself, the bird piercing time, will be new,
New yet the same, the same bird,
The same bird with the same body
(A bit worse for wear no doubt)
With the same soul
(A bit richer perhaps, like *coq-au-vin* on the second day).
You will be nearer your end.
Your end—what is it?
That is the question.
You think: Does my life simply end
Or will some great End gather me up?

You sit. Outside it is white.
Snow is falling, trillions and trillions of flakes—
The snow buries time.

You think: we are like flakes of snow.
But you realize that is nonsense.
You think: I live, the flake does not live, the flake will melt.
I will die—but to die is not to melt.
What is it to die?
Is it *not to be*, or is it *to be other*?
Who am I? What am I?
That is the question.
Shall I live?
You think: Only in Christ is there reason to believe I shall live.
Only in him did God undergo the shadow
And overcome it
And submerge it in light.
He is the flower in the cold.

You wake.
Everywhere it is white.
Snow heaps up on the window ledge,
Higher and higher.
You blow on a pane, the glass mists over;
You mark the mist with your finger;
Slowly the trace of your breath disappears.
It is white everywhere,
The whole world is white.
Snow is falling and falling.

Winter's Last Battle

A sharp breeze, gathering strength,
Strums the pine like a blues guitarist
And jangles the wind-chimes by the door of the stone house,
Demanding an ear:
"Hear ye! Hear ye!
Spring's back in force,
She's assaulting winter,
She's reclaiming the land!"
The flowering fruit trees,
Like a young woman waking to the meaning of her swelling stomach,
Spread the news quickly:
Leaves go chattering,
Blossoms go gossiping.
Suddenly everyone knows what's happening:
Spring is on the march.

The lordly chestnuts,
Lit up by a thousand white candles,
Knew all about it already.
Retreating winter, fearing their power,
Summons Wind to take them out.
The monster surges at nightfall,
Blasting the boughs.
The grand trees are galleons,
They breast wild waves,
Their white blooms are foam.
They battle and wallow for hours till Wind relents.

Now the houses in the hamlet come under attack.
The huddled stones take furious blows;
They wince to remember the ages
When they were sheltered inside earth's bowels.

The roof-nails strain to grip their tiles;
The hinges of the doors and shutters clench their iron fists;
The chimney breathes a prayer and makes its stand.
All the stars are gone out in the heavens,
The moon has fled.

But suddenly at midnight,
Winter,
Its strength spent,
Rage expunged,
Calls off Wind
And leaves the land.

Morning finds spring's legions still on a war-footing.
Cohorts of ragwort and fleabane are massed in the fields;
Daisies, nipplewort, yarrow, and hawkbit
Are standing tall on their stems,
Shields high;
Rank on rank of chervil and parsley line the waysides,
Lances raised.

But now Spring's Commander-in-Chief,
General Sun,
Informs all his troops the battle's done,
Spring has won.
Flowers and trees,
Bushes and shrubs,
Can lay down their arms.
And the order goes out across the land:
"Spread your fragrance,
Wave your rainbows,
You're free—
Sing!"

Harbingers

Spring bounds out of winter
Like a lion out of dark woods;
It rushes across the ploughed fields
Where mahogany cattle
Mirror the brown of the furrows.
Then it leaps into the trees and roars.

Colored plumes burst across the land
Like artillery explosions,
Flashes of pink and white,
Plum/cherry/apple
Purple
Tongue-pink magnolia
Foaming on the still-bare hills
Like champagne overflowing its glass:
These are scouts for the army of leaves
Preparing to invade the earth,
To inundate the land,
To glorify green.

Ten thousand yellow suns
Burning in the green grass:
Dandelions gazing
At their great big brother in the sky.
And now, a week gone by,
The suns are ghostly moons,
Ten thousand dandelions gone to seed:
Just puffy fluffs.
They gaze at their great big brother fluff
Floating in the daytime sky,
Floating on the navy lake high above them
Where the spring wind has blown it:
The dandelion moon.

O daytime moon,
Full-orbed,
You're a phantom buoy floating in earth's harbor—
To you earth's tides are moored,
O powerful *ghost*!

Now consider the speed with which a butterfly flits.
How can this *be*?
Or the just-hatched ordinary fly:
It zips around the house as fast as a bullet!
You think you see it zip
But you don't,
Not really.

Or consider a newly-minted lizard on a wall:
A millisecond and it's *up* the wall,
Down the crack,
Gone—
And you hardly saw it skitter!
The splay-toed little creature
Is as fast as a bird in the air,
As a fish in the sea—
How can this *be*?

And now consider the slug and the snail—
How wonderfully *slow*!
And the gherkin-headed, pointy-tailed turtle shuffling,
Its heavy shell a mobile mosaic:
Nature's tank—beware!

And now the earthworm—
Wrigglewrigglewriggle!

And consider the caterpillar moving slowly through the grass,
Its furry body humping and unhumping,
The *larva* of the swift-flitting
Drunkenly cavorting
Butterfly.

And now by night,
Glimpsed out of the corner of the eye on the kitchen wall,
Pasted on the plaster like a row of staples,
Then suddenly scuttling like a lizard—
Scuttling with the speed of a lizard—
A *millipede*.

Or perhaps—
Horrors!—
A gross *roach*?

How can these things *be*?

The Daily Circle

The sun rose like a marigold from under the earth
And bloomed. We were all gold.
Day stretched its arms and hugged the hills.
The trees shook out their hair.
Birds sang Handel.

Noon was stunning. A morning's toil
In a furnace deadens the nerves.
We were on the ropes, cross-eyed.
But food and drink put us back in the ring.
After a siesta, we came out swinging.

The sun sensed its decline.
It argued heatedly for two hours in mid-afternoon,
Lost the case, then planned its riposte.
The riposte came as it set a few hours later,
A conflagration that blew up the world.

The sun turned into a giant poppy
Floating on lava, a flower of fire.
The lava spewed out of the west
And inundated the sky; then it hardened
And the orange drained off, leaving the air ashen.

So the sun was dead. Yet it still lived
Where we couldn't see it, it rose to other eyes.
For us it was night, and we walked on igneous rock.
We had trouble sleeping, it was cold.
When the sun rose the next morning,
We leapt for joy.

Rain

Clovis and I are listening to silence.
The cat sits on his haunches on a wicker chair,
A napkin of sunlight is folded on his back.
Mother-of-pearl lines the grottoes of his ears;
Cascading swaths of brown fur sweep tail-ward.
His eyes are gold coins set in crystal balls:
Under sun's soft weight the lids slide closed.

We both sleep. We purr. Do we both dream?

We wake. It is raining. The sun has hidden.
Clovis yawns: his face becomes a mouth:
For seconds its roof is like an old-fashioned
Washboard, its tongue a pink wave. He blinks.
Both of us hear rain pattering. It patters
On the window-panes and roof, it pings
On the gutters. I go out on the porch to watch.
Clovis stays put. His tail switches back and forth.
He eyes me dubiously through the window.

Rain-noise and wet blur my senses. I watch.
On the patio-pool the drops make inter-
secting circles of ripples, wheels in wheels
Like gears meshing, a network of arcs.
The drops on the stone tiles splatter; on the ivy
They tick like hundreds of clocks; high up
In the sycamore their drumming is a susurrus
Sounding like rapids. I listen. I hear streams
Running in my boyhood. I am swimming,
Fishing. It is long ago. I dream and hear
The symphony of drops playing old tunes.
My heart lifts. Rain-smell takes me over.

I have smelled so many and so many rains

Time, where do you go? On the landscapes
Of our life you run your course. At day's end
We see that you have passed. You don't return.

Tears slide down the window-panes. Drops drum
On the flagstones, splash, plop. The sky is off-
white, the air like a sieve of gray mesh.
The gold of the marigolds is muted,
The begonia and roses washed out;
The trees have turned the color of pigeons;
Gray hangs on the pummelled earth, brooding.

Now rain-veiled tree-clumps emerge from the mist.
Light seeps through the water-ridden land.
The drop-patter slows, the gray tarp over us shreds.
Cloud-trains appear on invisible tracks
And shuttle through freight-yards of sodden air.

I awake. Have I been sleeping? I hear birds.

The rain has stopped. A fluttering in the chestnut tree
And big drops roll off the leaves and make geysers
In the patio-pool. Everything drips, drains.
A breeze flushes drops from the foliage,
Cool air soothes the porch. Bird-song swells.

I am here. It is now. The mind's afflictions
Cannot change that truth, I tell myself,
Nor the world's sorrow. This present is solid,
Though I may dream times past and future.
Life wells up; we sleep, wake; we move, we move
On. Sun's light melts encumbering grief.

Decay is less primordial than growth.

In bird-song is eternal laughter

Clovis is lying in the wicker chair asleep.
He opens his eyes as I come in. I scratch him,
He purrs. Here is where we sat and napped,
My cat and I, my brown beast, dear Clovis.

Yet I cannot refrain from asking:
Was that an hour past we napped,
Or once upon a time long ago?
Clovis eyes me testily and flicks his brown
Tail twice back and forth on the wicker chair.
I smile and stroke his pointed ears. He purrs.

The Hollyhocks

Hollyhocks rise above the old stone wall.
The flowers are fixed to stalks like mountaineers.
Faded blooms droop by yellowing leaves near the base;
Mid-way up, mature flowers fight their fears
Of the void they hang in and the long fall
To death if wind ripped them from the stalks;
Higher, young buds at the stalks' tips talk
Of conquest, thrust out rashly, climb space.
Beyond the wall children are splashing in a pool;
They shriek, jump, dive off the board, kick a ball.
Their parents watch anxiously. They see the race
That lies ahead. The grandparents sit in deckchairs
Calmly. They know the score. Through the years
They've run the course. They once were buds, bold
Blooms. Then they swelled along the stalk. Now age
Seres them. Yet still they anchor the climbers' rope.
Until their petals curl and fold, they'll wage
Life's war and bear the scent of hope.

Pride

Body-builder clouds flex their muscles.
They tower and glower.
Considering contemptuously the soft hills, they gloat.
They preen, boast, growl,
Smirk, snicker, stalk.
They will douse the hills,
Drown the land;
Their sword, wind, will rip trees,
Uproot orchards,
Destroy what men have made.
The sky will crack,
Day will turn to night.

Having shot their wad,
Having strained and strutted,
Having roared and bellowed,
The body-building bar-bell toting bumptious clouds
Will be spent.
Their bombast vented,
They will deflate like tires
And hobble bumpity-bump over the hills, muttering.
The sky will clear,
Then the sun will come out.
The blue day won't even remember the braggarts.
The green hills,
Made of rock under their soft curves,
Will laugh.

PART III

Cloud Sequences

I

The sky drew back its cotton clouds
And toppled out of night.
The bed was a rumpled mess,
Sheets pulled every which way.
It had been a hard night.
The rain started beating down at dusk.
The clouds went on a binge.
By midnight the sky was dead drunk.
The drops kept hammering the city streets
Like the hooves of wild horses.
The wind raged and swore;
The trees swayed like Bedlamites
And slapped heaven blasphemously.
Everything that could flap flapped,
Everything that could slam slammed.
In the wee hours, having wreaked havoc,
Wind took rain by the arm
And the two reeled away over the horizon,
Shouting raucously.
Sky pulled the clouds up over its head
And tried to sleep.
Dreams harried it:
Carnival figures with frightful masks
Cavorting in the air lewdly.
Day broke fitfully.
The sky drew back its sheets
And toppled out of night, red-eyed.
The bed was a rumpled mess.
The clouds, faces flushed with a dreadful hangover,

Scudded about aimlessly.
It had been a hard night.

II

Sky makes up its bed slowly.
The sheets are straightened,
The covers tucked in.
Light imposes discipline,
Night's hooligans skedaddle.
The clouds form patterns of white ripples:
Windrows in sky's hayfield,
Railroad ties on tracks
Bearing wind-trains to far-off places,
Horizontal ladders hung on air.
Order is restored.

III

As day develops in space-time,
Sun's heat and planetary winds—
The conjunction of innumerable pressures enabling belligerency—
Together transmogrify the ranks of ripples into armies,
Mighty battalions invading vast space
Like Napoleon's troops marching into Russia.
Advancing inexorably on air,
Propelled by mythical delusions,
The cloud-armies, like Napoleon's troops,
Confront contrary currents of force
And begin to unravel;
Retreating inexorably on air,
The battalions disintegrate.
As sun moves past noon,
Winds carry back across sky's burnt ground

Thousands of tattered cloud-bits,
Shredded ranks, straggling fragments,
Remnants of the invincible battalions.

IV

Light shifts key.
For a time, space softens.
A parade with fantastical floats
Takes form along sky's main boulevards.
Bulky cotton creatures glide by on invisible wheels:
Whales, hippopotamuses, zebras, elephants.
The sky becomes a many-ringed circus
Deploying cloud-acts in slow motion,
Mute performances enrapturing air.

V

Now thunderclouds are piling up on the horizon.
Sky's accumulated vapor builds billows
That rise above the distant hills like castles,
Flat-bottomed and sculpted by shadow,
Their towers and bulbous domes
Backlit and gilded by the lowering sun,
Muscle-bound masses threatening storm.
They loom, immovable.
Yet imperceptibly their shapes alter
As the sun's heat wanes.
The immovable is moved.
Slowly the towers evaporate like snowmen,
The storm retreats into the future.

VI

The celestial stage is being cleared,
Winds and the dropping sun
Are shifting the furniture.
Dense banks of mottled cloud
Sit atop a strip of pale blue along the southern horizon.
In several regions of sky huge slabs of shadow
Hang low above the earth like ceilings.
Elsewhere in sky's ocean
Continents are breaking into islands, archipelagoes, peninsulas.
Sun-shot blobs drift placidly overhead:
Pillows, antimacassars, cotton-stuffed cushions.
Gauze-films blanch the stage-set's northern reach,
Lacy swirls decorate the eastern vault,
Fluffs floating westward anticipate sunset.

VII

Across the sky pink flecks appear.
Trails of cloud begin to flush.
On the western hills pastels thicken into oils.
The dropping sun, marigold, goes orange, reddens,
Then settles like a huge tomato
On the cloud-bank covering earth's rim.
Slowly it sinks, as if swallowed.
Once out of sight under earth,
It lights a match like an arsonist
And sets the whole sky on fire.
The clouds burn dark red briefly,
Smolder, then go to gray ash.
Cooling, they contract and grow thin,
Then elongate into eels and lean fish
Swimming in the shoals of night.

Filaments on the horizon dissolve,
The hills go black,
Day's dome darkens.

VIII

The sky's stage is bare.
Night has come.
Bedtime.

IX

Venus smiles.

PART IV

The Plaque on the Bench

Tell on what far shore their eyes now gaze
That once beheld the same dark rocks I see,
These wave-wracked headlands, lizard-shaped, that graze
On wind and tidal draughts of fish-rich sea.
I'd thought them dead and gone for many a year;
Yet finding this old bench above the bay,
Its plaque displaying their paired names, I hear
Beneath the cries of gulls, the children's play,
The happy yaps of dogs at seashore's edge,
In the breezes riffling through the plangent pine,
The lime, the yellow broom—I hear a pledge,
Murmured, of solicitude, all divine.
Then—wondrously!—I sense them *present* here,
Their rapture bursting on the summer air.

For Richard Hays

At the heart of all your words is silence.
In the night of the world you hear bells
Chiming. It is silence you hear. You sense
Peace underneath earth's noise, wells
Of stillness far down under the daily slog
Through wetlands of knowledge, your life,
The tramp through swamps of books in heaps, log-
Piles, bogs of words, teeming, sweaty…And rife
Too with truth for those hearing beneath the buzz
Of ceaselessly concatenating syllables
The Origin, the Source who IS, who does
Unheard his work, generating multiples
Of being, infinitely, in silence.
His Word you hear. You hear inside night
Melodies mute to most ears, intense
Notes populating scores of starry light.

These you share with us in love, wise guide
To many, to me old friend most dear, seen
Too seldom in the long years, alas, this side
Or that of the ocean, yet in heart near, keen
Brother, in Christ mated long ago,
The night you sang to welcome Christopher to earth,
With joyful, wild chords greeting him: "Hello!"—
Young father exulting at your new son's birth.

Then Sarah, much-loved daughter—girl!—breaking
On life's stage—her heart, like yours, like Judy's,
Set to range God's wide creation seeking
That place—*hers*—to plant her tent, send melodies
Skyward, dance, deploy her lively art.

And Chris himself is father now. The years swing
Swiftly. Walk now with Judy to the end,
Listening to the silence. Sing to God, to us. Sing.
And you shall hear Him one day speak: "Welcome, friend."

Friends

I have been here before.
I have heard the songbirds pipe and flute
In the flowering locust trees.
I have seen them dart from branch to branch
Like black arrows
And perch among the leathery seed-pods
And clusters of white blossoms.
In the passing waves of wind
The branches sway like dancers on a shore;
The leaves adorn the maidens
With necklaces of shell
And bracelets of green glass.

How has the scene before me changed
Since I was here the last time,
Fourteen years ago,
Before moving to another country?
The songbirds are not the same songbirds,
The leaves are not the same leaves.
The girl who lived in the room
Behind the balcony where I'm sitting
Has grown up and left home.
Now other girls giggle at the swimming pool
And run along its edge, shrieking.
The beauty her mother was famed for in youth,
The daughter has claimed for herself.

The mother's face is lined now,
Her waist has thickened.
She is talking to my wife in the parlor
While I sit listening to thrushes.
The women are renewing their friendship,
Frayed by departure and distance,

Diluted by time,
Strained by misunderstanding.

Before the friction of life
Showed the toll it was taking,
These two were young women,
Their friendship was strong.
Where did they go to?
Young women, I address you,

You who often sat together
Where these two are sitting today;
Who talked about having children
And helping people in need;
About editing books,
Teaching French,
The lapse in moral standards;
About raising kittens,
Re-upholstering sofas,
Making *sauce Béarnaise*—
You who laughed so easily,
Who were so full of expectations
(As your mothers before you had been),
Until painful times of testing
Took the luster off the silver
And transformed zealous exuberance
Into persevering hope
(Your mothers are old now,
Their memories are failing,
Whole chunks of past time
Are dropping out of their minds,
Including friendships they cherished
When they were young women)—
Young women, where did you go?

To the far side of the moon?
The Andromeda galaxy?
Do you exist outside the memory
Of your existence?

We are here, we are here,
I hear the birds piping.
But how are you here?
We are here, we are here

Sun shimmers in the locust trees,
Painting the fissured trunks;
The blackbirds flit among the branches,
Weaving invisible skeins.

There I am, a dark-tanned boy
Thrashing down the outside lane in a swimming race:
I was out ahead but lost
Because my eyes were closed
And I hit the side of the pool
And stopped to see where I was.

Why that memory?

Who knows? Who knows? Who knows?

I'm sparring with Big Bill Matthes
After returning from summer holiday
With a notion I knew how to box:
A left to the head nearly floored me
And convinced me my future lay elsewhere:
I retired from the ring at age twelve.

Good for you, good for you, good for you

Now the crack of a bat on the windy field
Of Randall's Island:
The ball lifts up—
Can I?
Yes!
Run, run—Yes!—running, running—
Yes!—reach—stretch—yes!—
And it's there in the glove, secure,
And I slow, stop, shift weight,
Pivot, cock my arm, hurl—
And the ball streaks high into the air,
Looping over the blue back of the sky,
And carries all the long way to home base—
Wow!

Young boy, oblivious of past and future
(But pain already is etching shadows
On your heart, isn't it?)—
Who are you?
What have you to do with me?
I muse beside the pool, the ring, the ballpark,
As songbirds warble in the golden light.
Yes, I passed this way, that is undeniable.
But where did he go, that "I"?
Where is that dark-tanned boy?
Centuries have rolled over the world since he lived.
Is he still alive?

Come—we can't dawdle all day over this matter.
We must fish or cut bait.
Young boy, I will say this to you:
I do feel you inside me, in my bones
And in the blood that sings in my veins.
Your innocence and loss of innocence

Are both lodged somewhere near the base of my spine.
You live in more than my memory.
You are not lost, you have meaning,
You are not a shade in the land of the dead—
All this I will say to you.
You ask who you are?
Well, you have become who I am
And in me as I am here today,
You exist.
And because by God's grace
I shall live forever,
Forever becoming more fully
The person I am,
You too shall live forever,
Since without you I have no existence,
I am not who I am.

So there we have it.
I have chosen to fish.
One must face up to the issues.
My wife and her friend are doing just that
In the parlor. More power to them.
One mustn't let life get away from one.
The songbirds sing loudly.
They don't think about the tunes
They sang last year;
Somehow those tunes are part of the tunes
They sing today.
Of course, I admit,
It's not so simple as that,
Because songbirds don't think,
They just sing.

The locust leaves flutter
In the afternoon breeze;
The bracelets glitter,
Green dancers sway;
Blossoms snow down,
Filling the air;
Years vanish under the petals.

My wife knocks on the door
And joins me on the balcony.
"We had a good talk," she says, smiling.
"We've found each other again."

Happy you, happy you, happy you,
Sing the songbirds.
Happy you, happy you,
Happy you

The Friends Have Gone

The guests go,
the cars drive off,
voices fade into the past.
Now comes down quiet.
The palm tree trunks curve up
like the necks of giraffes.

Giraffes are feeding by the lake

By the lake purple lilac blooms.
Palm fronds bristle above the lattice of old toothed stalks
that have burst from their sheath of bark.
The palm fronds murmur and wave;
the lilacs, the sedge, the slew-grass by the lakeside,
the water-oaks, mimosa,
the long-needled pines—
everything waves to everything,
everything murmurs.
Shadows scrub the lawns.

In the lake turtles float,
legs spread out like the tabs one pulls to open boxes,
necks poking up above the water
like the necks of giraffes above acacia groves
on the plains of Africa.
Turtles crane their necks,
palm trunks curve up.

Giraffes are feeding by the lake

These objects gathered under this blue sky,
under these tufts of cloud,
keep in perpetuity the words spoken in time.

In this space now,
under these palms,
where giraffes of a thousand mornings feed,
I sit in solitude knowing loss
but also fullness as well,
looking backward
but also forward,
remembering,
anticipating
(I am not death's prey yet).

I hear again the voices of friends,
my wife's clear voice,
I hear the reassuring voice of my God:

I am with you
I travel on the wind
I travel in the sunlight and the flutter of bird-wings
In the rustle of squirrels' feet over dead leaves under the privet hedge
In the population of memories in your heart's secret nooks
I travel

All that exists, I make

I am with you
In you
I love you
Do not fear time
I am here
Today
Yesterday
Tomorrow

Such is the shape of quiet in the wake of convivial encounter,
the emptiness that follows the exchange among friends of laughter
    and words.
There is loss,
for the voices have dropped away in the past;
no fellowship of trees and waving green plants
can replace them.
Yet there is contentment too,
a thickness of experience,
the reassurance of continuity:
this moment, fathered by the past,
is great with future.

Remembrance joins with the Spirit of God
to invest the air and land and mortal creatures
with the virtual immortality of being.

Giraffes are feeding by the lake
Feeding in acacia groves in Africa
Under the capacious sky
They will feed forever

Waiting

I pace the roof of the Kigali airport,
Scanning the night.
I am alone on the roof.
The hall below is crowded with people waiting.
Up here it is dark,
There are few lights on the runway.
The sky is a black well,
There are no stars.
Will she come?

The plane is late.
Thoughts pace my mind,
Up down, up down.
I am a sand grain on the seashore washed by minutes,
Waiting.

Will she come?
Will grace drop out of the night?
My head is throbbing.
Here is where the genocide happened six years ago.
I am under a black tarp, suffocating.

Will she come?
Will she find my needle in the haystack of Africa?
Will she find my sand grain?
I wait.
I pace.
I pray.
Will my love come?

Suddenly I see a firefly far off in the night—
The plane!
A rumble—

The plane!
I tear down the steps to the arrival hall.
I join the lean black men in white shirts standing like pickets,
I join the black women in colored dresses standing like flowers.
Oh, we're an orchard waiting to be watered!

A door opens on the balcony above us.
A man appears, then a woman,
Then another man carrying a big bag.
They scan the crowd expectantly.
Two more women emerge, carrying baskets.
Their eyes roam the hall below.
Suddenly they point and gesticulate, laughing.
One by one all five hurry down the ramp.
The crowd parts, bodies jostle.
Shouts, hugs, laughter.
Everybody is talking at once.

Then two more men appear on the balcony,
Then another woman.

I wait.

Where is she?
Will she come?

Oh!
Oh—it's *she!*
Look! Look!
She's coming out, she's on the balcony!
Her *face*—
Her *white face* among all the black faces!
And her handbag—her beloved red handbag!
My love!

She sees me!
She smiles,
She waves.
I cry out: "Victoria!"
She makes her way down the ramp,
She elbows her way through the crowd.

Oh!
She is here!
We embrace—
Oh!

She has come.

The Temptation of Darkness

Out at the edge of starlight
I have peered into night's uncomfortable regions
And wondered at the plight of its denizens.
How can you know of their loneliness,
You who mask yours behind flickering screens?
How can you fathom Nature,
Who oppose truth with virtual smiles?

Here light is a faint blur,
Like the memory of a woman's face
On a street at dusk.
Those who live in night's climes
Are too rapt by Dark
To heed trembling stars.
Their eyes are riveted
By the cavernous black.
They can't imagine being kissed
By light's sensuous lips.

See that heart out there—
Like a lime-leaf spinning
In November's winds!
What branch held it once?
Where is its tree?
Its earth?
Where are the roots it drew from?
Oh, gone, gone, gone!
In November's winds the torn leaf tumbles,
No place to settle but the cold ground,
Cold leaves for friends,
All dying or dead.

And yet she knew summer's emerald once,
The lemon air of April,
The sand's gritty feel
At ocean's fringe.
She dressed dolls once,
Threw snowballs,
Decorated Christmas trees.

Later she kept a dachshund
And belonged to several committees.
In England, as a young woman,
She rode side-saddle and charmed squires.
Moonlit nights in that buried youth
Tasted like sherry.

Did she really throw snowballs once?

Do you see the crystal glasses and faience plates
Standing behind glass doors in cupboards
And on dressers of mahogany among platters
And porcelain vases, next to silver jugs
And teapots and fluted sugar bowls
Blazoning daylight on their polished sides?
All these garnished lives!
What lips quaffed the wine those goblets held?
What hands tapped rhythms on those white plates,
Delicately wielding forks and knives and shiny spoons
Like drumsticks?
Who knows?
The goblets haven't left their posts in years.
The crystal and silver gleam like stars,

Emitting light from brighter ages.

Life at the edge of night is memory

Yet the lady on the galaxy's corner,
Where enormous Dark lies brooding,
Remembers yesterday's long-gone light *today*.
Even now it strokes her face like fingers
And smoothes her hair like rain.
Oh, lady, look up!
Look towards the sociable light!
Those beams will keep your heart from tempting darkness.

Do you know the temptation of darkness?
It fixes the mind on a dot,
A black hole sucking life out of creatures;
All *other* is absorbed in its maw.
This is virtual reality's twin:
Nothingness.
Oh, may we turn
Let us turn
Let us
Turn
Towards the substantive stars,
Where love is.
There burns the infoliated rose
In endless combustion.

Pour Albert, Mon Frère Bien-Aimé

(whom, as he lies dying, I liken to the moon and to the Church)

When, moon, will you shake loose your coils
And stand untrammeled in the night,
Ready to exercise Adamic sway
As lord with Heaven's Lord, and His glad bride?

I've known you netted in the limbs of oaks
Like a flounder thrashing in a trawl;
Though free in Truth, and riding high beyond
Earth's bounds, to eyes you lay enthralled.

Shall I say it wasn't so, you *weren't*
Enthralled, since science claims the moon
Is neither fish, balloon, nor captured kite,
So can't possibly be tangled in a tree?

Is the moon, then, no slice of apple
On a porcelain dish? Is it no paring
Of the gods, no finger-nail of vain
Athena? Is it no fungus on the sky?

But hear again: I say I've seen this moon
Pathetic, not just free; seen it really
Caught in mesh and bleak barbed wire,
Trussed with power lines and skewering thorns.

Facts are like a map; but images
Evoke the grainy land itself,
The very rivers, valleys, hills and woods:
Wet, hot, hard, green, round.

Images carry the meaning of things.
And so I grieve, kind moon, for you—
When will you be free from pain? I see
You break on rock of cloud and buckle, stuck

On jagged reefs, canted starboard, knocked
By monstrous seas, hounds of hell
Slashing, raking: all night long you groan,
Drowned in spray and the seething foam of the ruck.

But look: change comes! Far off I see—
Where even imagery falters and the void
Contests the smile of God—the grace-touched
Moon appearing like the angel Gabriel!

I see it white, billowing on black,
Glorious in linen-light,
Loosed from earth's bedevilled coils
And the plunge and weltering wrack of cloud.

Emblem of Christ's Bride, the Son's Belovéd!
Image of the One who reigns!
See—a greater than John arises!
A greater than Gabriel!

O happy moon, saved from night
To be in night day's sign!
Your Lord has lifted you from gravity:
With Him you reign! With Him you shine!

Grief

You have slipped away, my dear,
You've left me all alone to weep;
My tears will bear your body off
While I cold vigil keep.

But though I weep five heavy years,
No grief will bring you back to me;
Your life has left my frame of time,
You've found eternity.

I crash against the emptiness
As though against a wall of stone;
No flint is harder than this void
That finds me here alone.

You seem to move across my sleep
Like footsteps on the cobbled walk;
I dream and think you've come again,
I wake, I hear you talk,

And then—O God!—no voice is there…
No old familiar hand appears
Behind the door; upon my brow
No fingers still my fears.

The sunlight takes me in awhile,
It warms the windows of my mind;
Then rain-clouds swing the shutters closed:
I grope bewildered, blind.

Worst of all to suffer, dear,
Is not the sheer, unbroken ache;
Pain that's pure I'll bravely bear
For you, for our love's sake.

The worst is when I flinch with fear,
Assailed by sullen stabs of shame:
"You failed to show how much you loved…"
Was I too shy? Too tame?

Did I not tongue enough my heart's
Delight, or carol loud enough
My joy that you were mine? I fear
My lips were often stiff.

O arms—did you embrace enough?
Hands—did you caress his hair?
Stroke his face? Did you convey
My hunger and my care?

No, no, no. Love, how short I fell
Of all I wished to be and do!
And now you're gone. Oh, see my grief!
May my tears comfort you.

Clovis

My dear God, we pass but you remain.
All those teeming on earth's face today
Will be elsewhere tomorrow. Where?
Our cat Clovis, our incomparable King Clovis,
Oh, our most, our most beloved cat, our Clovis,
Has died,
And we weepweepweepweepweep,
For everywhere we see him,
His sweet face, his whiskers so lovely,
Glass eyes of gold agleam with love,
Cocoa coat so soft to touch, so thick,
Black wet rubber nose so wonderful to rub—
Everywhere we see him: on the chair's arm,
The radiators, the suitcases in the car, our laps,
Stretched on the floor like a furry comma
As we enter our flat, so happy to see us,
To welcome us, to give us his love and have ours.
Everywhere we see him at Puy del Claux,
Jumping from the car, running up the stairs,
Sunning on the walls, prowling in the grass,
Leaping out the velux window,
Then glancing back at me,
Triumphant yet wanting reassurance,
Wanting my love, my affirmation—
Oh, Clovis, you have them!
Dear Clovis—how you have them!
How we love you!
How we affirm you !
Everywhere we see you—
And *nowhere*.
Your presence is absent. You are gone.
In this life we won't see you again,
And even though we believe with all our hearts

That we'll find you again
When we are raised to new life in God's Kingdom,
You being part of who we are forever,
For now you are gone,
You are gone from our side,
Death has taken you away.
Oh, dear furry brown "shaw", dear Clovis.
We weepweepweepweepweep.

The Canvas

A red ground, like his last painting, "The Concert".
And then Staël threw himself from his window in Antibes.
His body lay on the pavement by a streetlamp until dawn.
"*Je n'ai pas la force de parachever mes tableaux*,"
he had written to Jacques Dubourg, his art dealer.
So his end, a red ground.
And how would you say it is with us?
A slab of red applied with the knife,
Our age.
Slathers of thick paint in bands on earlier canvases,
Black cubes in piles,
Heaped blocks,
Masses poised, jumbled, seeking balance.
Oh, the trapezoids yellow like the gold of Byzantine icons!
The triangles of purple like the velvet of kings!
But so often crossed,
Scotched by fierce strokes,
Brown bars flung every which way like toppled pillars.
Already the end was in the beginning:
The catastrophic upheavals,
The unhealable wounds,
Loss of home, of parents, of language.
And so the red ground erupts through the ripped paint,
Blood pours through the sheared canvas,
Structures fracture,
Worlds crack,
The quest for equilibrium collapses.

(Ah, the gold cello in "The Concert"—
Staël, hear me: *Your cello will play forever!*)

Globs of black suck hope from the yellow,
Suck hope from the purple.

"Je n'ai pas la force de parachever mes tableaux."

It's over.

Staël, hear me : *Your cello will play forever !*

PART V

Harold the King

Looking at the Bayeux tapestry
Commissioned by Bishop Odo
(Who is often shown wielding his mace),
One knows these events really happened.
Over nine hundred years ago,
On King Edward's death, Harold,
Earl of Wessex, declared himself
King of England, despite his pledge
Of allegiance to William the Norman.
The angry Duke crossed the Channel
And routed Harold's Englishmen;
King Harold himself was cut down,
Who had feasted and drunk so recently
With William in France, and joined him
At Dol and Rennes against Conan.
We see the king on the tapestry
Under the green embroidered words:
"*Harold Rex, Interfectus Est*".
A horseman in mail, head lowered,
Delivers a thunderous blow, and Harold
Falls backward, lifeless and heavy,
As his battle-axe flies in the air.

He who here, on the linen sheet,
Shall suffer the blow of the Norman
As long as the tapestry lasts,
Did once take that blow in the flesh,
In a terrible battle on Hastings plain,
Fought on October 14
In the year 1066,
As shadows on the meadows of England lengthened.
Harold did not know his slayer,
Nor do we: that ruthless rider

Embroidered here, fiercely bearing
Down on the hapless king, felling
Him with a great blow, nine hundred
Years ago near the coast of Sussex.
On that day, in those seconds, Harold,
Mad with battle, oblivious
Of life and death, heard hooves pounding,
Sensed, perhaps, the weight and presence
Of a horse, glimpsed rider, sword,
The blade's flash: and it was over,
He was dead, a corpse on the ground,
Who earlier that day had given orders
To his knights and said his prayers;
Who—weeks, months, years before—
Had galloped at dawn hunting boar;
Drunk with his men in the great Hall
Hung with banners from older battles;
Lain beside his wife in bed,
Stroking her hair and breasts, as once,
In a time out of time, unimaginable,
He'd lain on his mother's bosom, a baby,
And sucked from her nipples the milk of life.

Harold is fallen;
He will hunt and drink no more,
Fight, hate, love no more—
He has gone the way of all flesh.

Nine hundred years later,
Looking at the Bayeux tapestry,
We see the events at third remove,
As a fiction, albeit historical,
And even though the lower border
Of the linen is littered with heads

And arms and arrow-pierced bodies,
We cannot take in the tragedy,
The suffering, shock and horror
(And we've seen so much since, haven't we?),
We only note the outward event
And the significance historians
Tell us it had, the way it changed
The course of history, etcetera.
And so it did, undoubtedly.
But for Harold and the mutilated
Knights depicted on the tapestry,
And for their wives, children, and parents,
The meaning of the catastrophic battle
On 14 October 1066,
When Harold's force was beaten
At Hastings and Duke William conquered
England, was very different
From what the earnest historians,
And even the artist who designed
This commemorative story, stretched
Out here on more than two hundred
Feet of linen, could ever express.
Unique and irreplaceable
Persons, stitched in the fabric
Of other lives, had been plucked
Up like threads from the weave, leaving
Unravelled hearts and homes
And the dark pall of loss and grief.

What common ground binds an event
With its representation in song
Or in narrative poem or picture?
Art distils emotion, gives it
Order, making sense of matter

In the raw; it works on another
Plane from flesh and blood, neither
Copying nor replacing
What is lived. Its deliverances
Are for the living, not the dead.
The dead have their reward, according
To their deeds and God's justice.
From Him they receive honor, or fail to.
If He does not remember Harold,
As a person made in His image
For whom He sent His Son to die,
Then the man figured on the cloth
At Bayeux did utterly perish
When the horseman struck him down
So long ago on Hastings plain.
Art can do the dead no good,
Nor can it save the artist himself.
He lives on in his work, some say;
But if only his work lives on,
How is he, as a man, better off?
Art can't confer immortality.

If I reflect on Harold's death,
It's on my own death I'm reflecting.
I won't die on the plain of Hastings
On October 14 1066,
And I may not die violently
In a battle that changes history:
But a day will come when, like Harold,
I too will be felled by death's blow,
And the few still living who walked
Beside me will soon go my way.
The memories of all I've done
And seen in life, of all I've been,

Locked up like buried treasure
In my heart, unknown for the most part
Even to my wife and dearest friends,
Will pass forever from this world,
And the spot where the flower grew
And flourished will know it no more.

We have no time for make-believe.
"If the dead are not raised, let us
Eat and drink, for tomorrow we die."
Thus Paul. If Christ was not raised,
The dead are not raised either—
And tomorrow we die.

But Christ was raised—Hallelujah!

In this life sorrow wraps its coils
Around us like a giant boa;
Our blighted world's a battlefield
Like the bloody plain where Harold died.
If there is hope, its source must lie
Beyond ourselves, in the mercy
Of the One who bequeathed us Life
By dying, who forgave our sins
And faithlessness, our pride, fear,
Bitterness, jealous hate,
And broke the fateful spiral
Of revenge and ceaseless war.

Envoi

"Rebels to your love, Lord,
We're bound to die—
Cleanse us by your blood:
Have mercy on us, gracious God.

Ravaged by the clenched fist—
The ancient lie—
We come naked, unshod:
Have mercy on us, gracious God."

Crater Lake

I

Barbarians mass on the border,
Blood in their eyes,
Like storm-clouds over mountains,
Brooding and horrible.

Fire and lust in their bellies,
In their hands steel swords;
Thunder in their mouths,
In their hearts rage, fury.

The horsemen plunge forward,
They slash, howl, hurl torches,
There is fire in the mountains,
The plains are aflame.

The riders come pounding,
The earth screams, turns orange,
They plunder the mountains,
They trample the prairie.

All living things scatter,
Brute beasts, birds, humans,
Men, women, wild creatures,
They all flee in terror.

Trees burst, pine, fir, cedar,
Green juniper blazes,
The hills turn to ashes,
Smoke strangles the air.

Earth, sky, rock, melt.
Humans, beasts, all bones.
The moon a head, severed.
Tree-snags supplicate heaven.

The fierce riders have vanished,
The hoof beats have faded.
The sun crumples in blood,
The cold mountains whimper.

II

Out of what hell comes such fury?
Clouds, lightning, are innocent—
But not the horsemen,
Not the horde,
Not we.
We are the horde.
Whence this rage in our hearts?
Not God, but craving to be—
Is that it?
So we ravage what is not of our making,
What is not of ourselves we destroy.

III

Narcissists greedy for glory,
We adore our reflection,
Drink the lake where it glitters:
Such is our Fall.
We drag the earth with us,
Make it new in our image,
Replace God with ourselves.
Enraged by our limits,

We ricochet madly,
Like squash-balls of rubber
In a four-walled court.
Our desire to master
Is God's gift, our vocation;
The will to possess,
Our perversion.

IV

Man's rage is like magma
Heaving everything upward.
We're a mountain erupting,
A convulsive volcano.
In place of a crown, behold, now a crater,
In place of soil, cinder.
Hot lava, bubbling,
Buries the earth.

V

Snow and rain fall,
God's Love comes down.
A lake forms in the crater,
Its blue mirrors heaven.
Thus set in our heart

(Once fractured by fire),
The blue jewel sheds beauty,
Transforming our wound.
Under sun's rapture,
In liquid of silence,
Pure token of mercy,
It shimmers with glory.

"There is a World Elsewhere"

I

When I hear wind shrieking
Round the corners of the house
Like the fury of an old man
Railing at his cracking bones,

I think of blizzards tearing
At the neck of ancient mountains,
As if to snap with cold
The dark granitic hold

Of eternal rock; I think
Of thunder and the weeping clouds
Harried by the brutal air
And ripping wolves of wind;

I think of cliffs that breast
Inquisitorial storms
And brook the knock and slap,
The punch and rake of seas;

I think of stars that fling
Their flames in human eyes,
Lighting fathomless night,
Until they cool and shrink,

Until the sun grows dark,
The seas turn cold,
The bright clouds fade,
And the planet closes down.

II

There is a structure makes
The world cohere and gives
Us ground to plant our feet
And work and eat and sing.

We build upon a base
Embedded in an order that endures.
No rage can overthrow
The limits put by God

Upon creation. The rock
And sea and wind subsist
In mutual dependence.
Change is patterned in a frame

And logic and a tension set
In place to bring forth life
And love and the freedom of the wild
Heart swelling in the green

Of June, when the scent of rose
And lavender and mint,
The nostril-biting smell
Of ocean and the smell of rain,

Invade the nerves and launch
The soul beyond the clay,
Beyond our mortal frames,
To realms of measureless joy.

III

What lightness is here—what breath!
It pumps deflated lungs,
Brings blood to sallow skin,
Makes bent backs straight;

It jigs like merry wind
In poplar trees, drifts
Like clouds that kiss the fields
With wine-dark lips, gongs

Like cowbells on the summer hills.
Now far now near, it bobs and
Echoes, in valley shade
And sun, on tides of air.

IV

The wind that sweeps the earth
Is borne by greater Wind;
The cliff that stands against
The sea is set in Rock

That waves cannot erode;
The cloud-surf breaking on the reefs
Of sky tells wondrous tales:
"There is a world elsewhere!"

Stampede

One day, bent double on a dirty rug,
My hand like an anteater's proboscis
Raking with a wet sponge the grime of cities,
Foul grit, rollers like gray worms, the tracked-in filth
From numberless shoes flapping on pavement,
I found my mind hurtling on a galaxy's back
To time's edge, riding radiating power
Like a cowboy on a bronco gyrating out of a chute,
A jockey on a stallion heaving out of a starting gate—
There I, clinging for dear life to incandescence,
To *white* a-blaze, stars singing like angels,
And all about me, pell-mell in space,
Rushing horses, millions, a tumultuous cavalry,
The riders hanging on for dear life to their mounts,
Manes flaming, tails straight out like comets,
All streaming together into nothing,
White pouring into black,
Stampede of stars at time's edge,
Being erupting—

Glory

And I, bent double on the Persian rug,
My hand like an anteater's proboscis,
Go on raking rollers and the urban grit
To help my wife clean up the flat for guests,
While the city below contorts and howls,
Honking, flashing, roaring, bawling.

And at time's edge the horses hurtling hurtling

                              hurtling

A Far Country Here

The snow has melted.
White covering everything has gone—
White, a sign of somewhere else,
A far country enfolded in love.

The snow melted on the stones first,
On the stepping stones and the granite slab in the garden.
(Stone holds sun's heat.)
On the grass and fields,
Under cold's dominion,
White lingered.
But now green and brown are back.
The walls of white along the branches all have fallen down.
The trees write their ordinary script on the sky again,
The princely flourishes are gone.

The sun is back too.
Pools on the paths are blue,
Ennobling the mud.
Passing clouds admire themselves in the puddles.
The berries in the bushes have lost their snow-caps,
The dry leaves have taken off their coats.
Sun-squares slide across the walls in the houses again:
Gold on wood, beige on stone.

The silence too has thawed.
Under snow, the earth was still,
Even the air held its breath.
Now birds are peeping again.
The thaw is like fire in the hearth, *taking*.
It renews *here*.
The white told of a far country.
(Was it *eternity*?)

Yet that country seemed *present*,
Everything under snow,
Everything under fresh white sheets.

Now we're back home again
Amongst the greens and browns.
But the white in my memory is like home too—
A far country *here*.
In my heart it keeps company
With the greens and browns.

The Ridge

I

I would know this ridge with words.
I would penetrate its being
As sense cannot,
As words alone can do,
Words and paint.
No, not quite so
(These words need amending):
Truly you may intuit the ridge's being
By considering its beauty,
Passing from observation—
Including analysis—
To love.
Through sense,
As impressions touch the heart,
You may find union with this ridge,
Claim as yours the gold light creeping up its flank
As sun sinks westward,
The shadows deepening below.
But others cannot share this union,
It is yours alone,
A private ecstasy.
But words—
And paint—
Appropriate otherwise.
Here a world is projected beyond you,
Outside of you and the ridge,
Of your union in love,
Where that love's *meaning*—
The truth of the ridge in its created splendor—
Finds a form of its own,

Making the ridge's being *present*,
Or nearly so:
Present
Symbolically,
Present
Sacramentally
(In a sense),
Objectively—
Not by mere description
(Imitation can't bring *being* into presence),
But by music,
The word sung,
Images resonating across syllables,
Metaphors that orient the senses to move from the object—
This ridge here now—
To signs re-presenting it—
Pigments and signifying ink-marks—
Of which the power
(Beyond description)
Evokes *being*
(Beyond description).

II

The ridge in winter rises from the river.
Red dawn hails the ragged crest,
Light trills in the tree-tops,
Myriads of naked branches quiver.

Pin-cushion stuck with sycamore trees,
Its cloth ochre leaf-mold,
Folds of rock, up-heaved, in swatches,
The broad ridge slumbers in winter's freeze.

It stands stiff, rigid. Winter mirrors death.
Hibernating animals
Simulate dying. Life is
Underground. Sap drives rootward. Earth's breath

Blows cold. The wind slapping the ridge's face
Is cruel. The dark season frowns.
Brief days shorten time.
Nature slows to death's own torpid pace.

Hunkered against sky, great roundy hedgehog,
Splayed quills pricking azure,
The scraggly hill bristles in space,
Its brown bulk splashed with melting fog.

Roots grip the outcropped stones like hawks' claws,
Moss paints the slabs. Color—
Out of place on the dun ridge—
Hides among dead leaves and somnolent rocks.

III

But see—a cardinal ignites the woods:
Yellow light flushes the steep slope,
Squirrel tails ripple on the branches,
Birds skewer the tree-skeins and sun-floods.

A surge across the ridge, a rush in the ash,
Breezes in the oaks' dry leaves;
Pine-trunks creak, bark rubs on bark,
Woodwinds sing and sigh in the waking brush.

IV

Now, later, snow falls slowly down.
White cloaks the lumpy slope.
The snow smoothes rocks, chalks the trees.
The hill is soft, still. Whiteness. Hush. No sound.

The woods are quiet. The pied trees wear
Their snow like new-bought clothes.
The shaggy pines sport mittens.
Twigs, tickled by wind, fill the bright air

With soundless billows of snow-dust, white
Laughter drifting like mist
Through the motionless tree-boughs:
Shadows of angels, flutterings of light.

The calligraphy of trees under snow
Carries messages from heaven:
Networks of looping lines
In sepia ink are signs to earth below.

V

Night has stolen over the snow-bound hill.
The ridge looms, huge, asleep
Against the stars. At its foot
The river whispers. Midnight. All is still.

In this silence, *being* breathes. The zest
Of day gives place to quiet.
Here, mystery disrobes. Unveiled,
The Word simply *is*: creation now at rest.

PART VI

A Far Isle

I

Spray on a far isle
Licking the dark shore,
Old outcrop of granite
Battered by breakers;
Slow motion ocean
Flinging white blossoms
On flat-needled hemlock,
Blooms flying landward,
Phantoms of foam:
Quickening—briefly!—
(Do I dream? Do I live?)
Apprehensions of joy,
Of ripe love's white flame
In God's laughing eyes:
Recovery of time.

Unheard the waves' roar
Pounding the far shore;
Unheard the foam's hiss,
Froth's lingering kiss
Across the rock's dark back;
Unheard the sea-surge,
The roar up the granite verge
Of hungry water;
Unheard the old years,
Things done once,
Water coursing swiftly once,
Now frozen in time.

II

Youth's melodies muted,
Its bright dance a pantomime:
Quick-quick—
Click of shoes
Tossing hair
Dresses
Eyes a-gleam—
Gems—
Hands grope
Bodies clutching
Clumsy—
Ah, youth swept by
Unnoticed,
Self-obsessed,
Unconscious of time.

III

The middle years too
Have fallen mute,
The busy, muddling years:
The marrying
Struggling
Teaching
Travelling
The organization of life
Bills—
One tries to cope,
To love.

Those years had a different way of flying by:
they spun faster and faster

and then we began to notice how fast they were passing
because we were trying to accomplish something
something we couldn't define very well
something that seemed always just out of reach
and we weren't managing it
because there was no time—
our busyness had filled time up—
there was no time left

Those days swept us up
And rolled over us like waves.
Suddenly the children were grown up,
Gone
Suddenly our parents were lying in coffins
Or contained in urns the size of water jugs,
Gone
Our childhood receded like a dream;
Our future flickered like the shadow of a candle flame
on the stone pillar of a church.

IV

The spray on the far isle lifts and falls,
Slowed by miles of air;
The waves lurch, break, tumble.
We see the granite holding firm
Under the sea's lash,
We see the hemlock standing tall,
Sentinels of time;
But of those old dramas
That happened ages ago
(Or not even so long ago),
We hear nothing now.
We do not hear the surf's roll the waves' rush

Anymore
We do not smell the salt the pine the juniper
Anymore
Even the echoes are muted
So that we hardly even know we hear nothing
Anymore
Only our words try to reach back
The hands of words
Hands trying to touch bodies
Find faces
Trying—
Failing—
To *hear*

Yet suddenly the wind
Carries echoes to our hearts,
Sweet, wrenching echoes,
And then, as our loss presses in,
We stand stunned, as if stabbed,
As if dying—
And we are dying
For an instant we *do hear*
And, hearing, *do know*
That what we are hearing will not return in this life—
The exaltations, the sweet intimacy—
That it is *gone,*
That what it was exactly will never be again—
Never—
That its intimations of boundless communion
Will never be fulfilled in this life—
Never—
That the years left to us are few,
That we must live them ardently,
We must be kind, honest, loyal—

Give no time to bitterness,
Give no time to regret—
We must love:
For we see death racing towards us swiftly,
Leaning landward like a tidal wave,
Galloping like the shadow of the moon erasing the sun.

V

And the young pass by, insouciant.
They wear their shirts outside their jeans, nonchalantly—
Cool
What will they remember
When the time for remembering comes?
(We remember only what was *real*,
When some authentic connection
With reality outside ourselves
Was experienced.)

Perhaps they'll remember
More than I,
Perhaps they'll remember
More than I

The smiles on their faces,
The arms round each other's necks,
The skipping feet,
The fragile laughter—
Oh, may these be *true*!
May they be tokens of time reclaimed!
And may what they signify

Rise up forever
In the dance on that granite isle,
Where—night, day, night—
The breakers pound and boom,
The wild spray leaps and soars,
And white foam hisses joyously
Across the rock's dark luminous back.

The Yellow Rose of England

"The Yellow Rose of England" he called you.

Oh, what a gift she was to you, father,
My dear father,
My brave father much-medalled for heroism in the Second World War.
I cannot imagine how it would have been for you without her.
She found you in the Canadian wilderness,
A man's man strong like an oak,
Wild but with a heart wanting to be tender.
She found you with seven teeth knocked out by a wrench
When you made a false move working under a tractor.
The rest were yanked out later by a diligent dentist,
So that you looked for a time like an old man,
You looked like Popeye,
Until the dentures arrived from Vancouver
And you became Adonis again.

Oh, in those backwoods you were found and lost both,
Quaffing solitude,
Enduring loneliness.
Sometimes on quiet winter evenings—
The chores done, the cattle fed, Bossy milked,
You sitting pensive by the pot-bellied stove
In the new log cabin built with pine trunks
You'd cut and peeled and hauled with horses by yourself
Out of the evergreen forest you were cradled in—
Sometimes on quiet winter evenings
Your heart would fly out over Prout Meadow
Where the willows by the creek were thick
And the slew-grass in summer was shoulder-high,
Your heart would fly out and bend eastward,
Cross miles, cross years,

And come to rest beside your son in New York,
Back East where you lived in the crazy Thirties before the War,
In the Big City where the lovely Felice Rosen captured your heart,
Felice your first love,
Felice my half-Jewish mother raised in France.
Oh, she was exotic!
And *you* were Adonis!
For a time you were happy,
Happy in the crazy Thirties,
Happy for a few short years until things fell apart,
Until everything fell apart,
Until war broke earth's back.

And somewhere in the middle of all that I came into the world

You were off to Europe in the Office of Strategic Services,
You jumped into Yugoslavia behind the German lines
And performed bold feats,
Feats you volunteered for as your father had done in an earlier war.

You should have died several times but somehow didn't

You came home after General Alexander awarded you
The British Military Medal for Bravery
To find me your little son five years old,
And you stood *oh so proud* beside me in Central Park holding my hand,
You a handsome sergeant in your uniform,
Your little son in a winter jacket with a hood,
Unspeakably happy but a little lost too.

And then you headed west to join your mother and brother
In the wilds of northwest Canada

So your little son's heart broke a third time without his really knowing it,
And your heart broke a third time and you knew it,
But you were a *man* and had to put that out of your mind and think of a future,
Some kind of a future,
Some kind of a future where maybe your little son could be included somehow.

I visited you two years later when I was seven.
My grandmother fetched me in New York.
Five days and nights to cross the continent by train,
Three thousand six hundred miles
From the Big City to northern British Columbia.
We lived all summer in a tiny cabin with a hired hand:
Two big men and me.
You were my father, I was your son.
You found me, I found you.
For three months we lived together in a tiny cabin.
We were happy.
Then I had to leave and go back East.
I lost you for the fourth time.
I didn't see you again for six years.

And in the meantime you found your second love

English, restless, brave like you,
Gathering all the gifts of her race into one strong woman,
A man's woman,
A match for you,
A gift for you.
She found you on her way back to England from Australia
After separating from her own first love;
She found you in your mother's house in Vanderhoof

When you were in town getting supplies.
 As a reporter she'd come to interview your mother,
Widow of a famous man, your father, my grandfather,
Admiral Richmond Pearson Hobson,
Naval hero, former Congressional representative from Alabama,
Recipient of the Congressional Medal of Honor.
The English reporter rang the bell of Frontier House,
Expecting to find an elderly lady.
You opened the door—and *behold*:
There stood Adonis, snaggle-toothed!
You ushered her in with a smile,
You made of your teeth a laughing-point,
You charmed the English reporter.
She loved you right off,
You loved her right off.
Once your false teeth were in, you got married.

You took her home to your ranch,
You showed off your cabin, your hay-barn, your cattle,
Your big red tractor and yellow baler.
You were funny, you told tall tales, you made her laugh.
You taught her about the wilderness,
The first snows in November,
Everything white for five months,
The stars in the night sky frozen until break-up in April.
She got used to forty degrees below zero Fahrenheit.

Neither Birmingham nor Sydney had ever been like that

And she was smitten.
She loved you and she came to love the wilderness.
She got a job as teacher in the little schoolhouse three miles from
    the ranch.
She loved all the children and they loved her.

The Yellow Rose of England flowered!

And the Rose had a lovely scent.
You breathed it in day after day,
And your soul grew quiet.
You and your blond Rose both found rest
In the middle of the harsh North—
You found *stillness*.

Your Yellow Rose of England civilized you.
Your wildness mixed with sophistication from your New York days
Tantalized her;
Your sheer, blunt, unapologetic maleness excited her.
She admired you.
Yes, you *did need* handling,
Lots of handling—
And she learned how to do it.
It delighted her.
She was *woman* fulfilling her role,
Civilizing man.

And I, your son, found you again the next summer
When I came out again from New York to visit;
And you, my father, found me again after six years.
You were manly and strong, I looked up to you.
You took your teeth out and I doubled up laughing.
You taught me how to milk a cow, swing an axe, drive a tractor,
Shoot a rifle, ride Paint bareback, catch trout.
You showed me off to everybody when we went into town.
You called me "Teeney".
"This is my son Teeney", you'd tell your frontier friends.
"He lives back East with his mother, he's here for the summer."
They gave me a strong handshake: "Welcome, Teeney!".
You were proud, I was proud.

The Yellow Rose of England taught me to cook.
She taught me to pick mushrooms in the woods after rain.
She was a second mother to me.
She loved me as your son,
She loved me for myself,
She loved me as the son she never had.

For three months we were happy together

Then we awoke from the dream.
I said goodbye to the Little Creek, to Bossy, Paint,
The dogs Moose and Wampus.
I put on my city clothes.
You and your Yellow Rose of England,
Your second love,
My second mother,
Drove me ninety miles to the airport in Prince George.
We said goodbye on the tarmac.
As the plane lifted and headed East
You stood together side by side on the tarmac waving.
You waved and waved until I lost you again,
Until I lost you from view,
You and your Yellow Rose of England.

The Figure at the End of the Pier

Far off, at the end of a pier,
A lonely figure.
Water laps against the barnacled piles:"*slap-slap-slap*".
The sea is wrinkled like an old man's face.

A child comes running towards the lonely figure.
The man takes the child in his arms.
"I'm so glad you've come," he whispers.
"Perhaps now in my age you'll find comfort,
The assurance you missed as a child.
Perhaps your vigor will gladden me,
I'll feel less alone;
We'll take heart together,
Old man and child."

The solitary figure continues:
"I left you a long time ago for a far country.
Our mother was somewhere out there,
We never really found her.
Our father met another woman and was happy.
I met a wonderful woman too—Victoria.
She filled up my loneliness.
But we never had a child like you.
There's an empty place in my wife's womb,
There's an empty place in our hearts.
As a child, you didn't have a family;
As a man, I didn't have a family either.
What a joy if I'd been a father!
What a joy if I'd made my wife a mother!
Ah, what a mother she'd have made!

It was not to be.
Oh, my beloved and I roamed the world together.
We saw suns rise,
We saw suns set.
We weathered storms.
Ours was a great love.
But in our hearts there was that empty place.
The crib in the baby room was empty.
Inside our love there was a loneliness.
Victoria thought sometimes she felt a baby in her womb,
Or heard crying in the baby room;
But there was no one.
The crying she heard was in her heart—
The baby room was empty.

Yes, we found comfort in our Lord Jesus.
The sorrows of this life will give place to joy when we see Him face to face.
We'll know a plenitude unimaginable here.
We know that.
And you, little boy, who is *me* long ago—
Who is me that summer when you were seven
And joined our father for three months on his ranch
(A little disheveled kid in shorts with a bruised knee,
Gripped—in the photo—by Daddy's strong hands on your shoulders
After you'd fallen off the roof of our grandmother's house)—
Little boy, you bring comfort to me now,
Now as I hold you in my arms as if I were your father.

Let me tell you something:
Victoria has always known you, somehow.
Perhaps, somehow, you have been the child she never had.
And perhaps, somehow, in my age, I've been a father for her,

As well as a husband.
Perhaps.

Anyway, dear one, you are loved: by me, by her, by God. I'm happy you've come home."

Bees Among the Plums

I

Dark is creeping from the East,
Low clouds shut the door on the sinking sun.
A few bees drift among the plum trees like memories,
Then they are gone suddenly somewhere.
Late birds speed through the soft air, nest-bound.
Doves coo Vespers responsively.
Somewhere in the dusk
A nervous dog barks at the encroaching dark,
Then gives up.
Silence.
Gray turns to black.

II

Ask yourself, the air cooling:
Have the doors closed on your sun?
Have the plums lost their taste?
And home?
Where is home?
Where is the speeding bird going?
Are you barking in the dark?

III

Rise, heart!
See the young moon up there on her deckchair
Surveying the fecundity of stars,
A playground of children squealing with light.
She knows she will soon be great with child,

She will be filled,
Fulfilled.
Then she will rejoice with the stars.

Rest, heart.
Be blessed.

"Be still and know that I am God."

Old Man Under the Night

I stood like an old man under the night
With all the stars sprinkled across heaven like crystals.
I seemed to hear them tinkle like sheep-bells
Far off in the earth-warm fields
Where the sheep were settling down to sleep
In night's cavernous barn.

I saw the Big Dipper scooping up space
And its handle curving toward the bowl of the Little Dipper
Scooping up space, both Dippers hung in the void
As they were long ago when I stood wide-eyed,
A young man, and the old world too
Seemed young then to my eye.

I stood under the night like an old man
And saw a shooting star streak across the black
And go out like a spark somewhere out there,
And the Dippers motionless meanwhile,
Scooping out black space
Forever and ever.

I remembered I was once a young man
And went to and fro, here and there, like a firefly
Flitting about in the air everywhere
In the night, unconscious of time,
Till one day I was aware suddenly
Time was slipping by.

And it was like patterns of clouds at sunset—
You see the patterns changed but not the change itself;
And it was like waves seen from a plane high up—
You don't see the waves actually breaking,
Only the foam on the sea's face,

The waves having broken.

I stood under the night, an old man, and saw
My life a shooting star having streaked across heaven,
Persons and places fixed fast in the field
Of time past, like the stars in the Dippers,
And I seemed to hear them tinkling faintly
Like sheep-bells in the night.

Under the immense night I stand now, an old man,
And contemplate the nature of eternity.
Shall I not go out soon from this starred cave
Into light-filled Day, where change
Isn't loss, where once is now,
Where all good is present?

Shall I not stream with the persons I've cherished
Through reaches of creation unimaginable now?
The field of time will be a field of love,
The young will be wise, the old, young,
Constancy of life will prevail,
And ceaseless communion.

The Little Green Vessel

One evening, when the gulls circle over the islands,
they'll not find me anymore watching them, enchanted.
The keel of my mortal life will have been raised up,
my boat hauled onto the beach,
my days sailing the polluted seas of modernity,
ended. Where my little green vessel,
scarred and scored within and without,
stood before the wind, breasting the waves,
or tacked between the cultivated islands,
or ventured now and then upon the boundless waters,
there will be found only empty ocean.

Perhaps someone will wonder where the sailboat went
that used to ply the waters near the islands,
in which a man, enchanted, sat every evening at the tiller,
watching gulls glide down the darkening air
and cry against the coming night.
The gulls will not feel my loss,
though I loved them, their wildness, their beauty.
But perhaps their raucous cries over the islands will be sadder,
the dark waters where they circle, lonelier.

Over the horizon, beyond reach of the gulls,
I shall be plying purer seas.
You need not weep, O dear ones,
O most dear one.
God will have healed the cracks in my heart;
my soul's cross-currents will be a single stream
flowing with Love's force beyond time.

O dear groaning creation, do not despair:
on the promised Day when the Lord Christ comes to claim you,
your polluted waters will be purified,

your fissures and crevasses filled,
the poisons in your earth leached out.

Here where I sail now in effulgent Light,
my green vessel rocks on gentle seas
in the company of innumerable vessels of all shapes and sizes
that spread out towards infinity like galaxies in space.
You will join me soon, O most dear one,
and we shall be gathered into one great Love
by the Captain of the fleet, in whom all good
that was once, all truth and beauty, are *now*.

www.ingramcontent.com/pod-product-compliance
Lightning Source LLC
Chambersburg PA
CBHW070501100426
42743CB00010B/1718